Praise for DEMO

"Gone are the supervillains and secret schools, and instead you have the things real teens care about: friends, first loves and the need to get away from everyday life. It's less bombastic than Wood's run a few years back on Marvel's Generation X but it is scarier and much more human than mainstream comics usually dare to be. Grade: A" **VARIETY.COM**

"...wonderfully different... what the X-Men would be if they were created today." **COMIC BOOK RESOURCES**

"...like watching a good piece of indie film"
LIQUID EXPERIMENTS

"Lacking recurring characters, DEMO altogether is less reminiscent of other comics series than of a thematic rather than continuous-narrative novel... High praise, maybe, but deserving."
BOOKLIST, starred review

"...the most human comic-book series on the market today"
THE FOURTH RAIL

"...compelling..." **NINTH ART**

"DEMO is currently ruling my entire universe"
SAN FRANCISCO BAY GUARDIAN

"The stories in DEMO are incredibly diverse... about the rotten-ness and the wonder of being young, the endless redemption available and the endless difficulty of achieving it... There isn't a single story here that I didn't love, that didn't make me think, that didn't thud home in my heart" **BOING BOING**

"Wood creates really mature comics... because his characters find themselves having to grow up and see the world in entirely new ways." **TEEN PEOPLE**

"Buffy the Vampire [Slayer] fans will be right at home as the problems of teen angst manifest themselves as super-powered metaphors." **IGN.COM**

*SELECTED FOR THE NEW YORK PUBLIC LIBRARY'S
"BOOKS FOR THE TEEN AGE" 2007*

DEMO

WRITTEN BY

Brian Wood

★

ILLUSTRATED BY

Becky Cloonan

SPECIAL THANKS TO RYAN YOUNT

Cover design by Brian Wood
All artwork by Becky Cloonan
Publication design by Amelia Grohman

DEMO

Published by DC Comics. Cover, text and compilation
Copyright © 2008 DC Comics. All Rights Reserved.
Originally published in single magazine form as DEMO 1–12.
Copyright © 2003, 2004, 2005 Brian Wood and
Becky Cloonan. All Rights Reserved.
All characters, their distinctive likenesses and
related elements featured in this publication are
trademarks of Brian Wood and Becky Cloonan.
VERTIGO is a trademark of DC Comics.
The stories, characters and incidents featured
in this publication are entirely fictional.

DC Comics
1700 Broadway, New York, NY 10019
A Warner Bros. Entertainment Company.
Printed in Canada. First Printing.
ISBN 13: 978-1-4012-1621-4

Contents

1

HEY, YOU EVER GET THIS *WEIRD* FEELING THAT YOU'RE *DIFFERENT* SOMEHOW?

EH?

YOU KNOW, LIKE THAT YOU HAVE SOMETHING SPECIAL, AN *ABILITY* OR *PHYSICAL TRAIT* OF SOME KIND THAT SETS YOU APART FROM EVERYONE ELSE?

BUT, LIKE, YOU DON'T WANNA *TELL* ANYONE, IN CASE YOUR FAMILY AND THE REST OF SOCIETY GETS FREAKED OUT AND TREATS YOU WEIRD, ALL *PREJUDICED AND SHIT?*

YOU KNOW WHAT I'M TALKING ABOUT? YOU KNOW THAT FEELING?

YEAH, I DO.

"NYC"

THE SUBURBS.

ONE YEAR EARLIER.

MARIE! COME TAKE YOUR PILLS!

MOM, I'M LATE FOR SCHOOL! AND MIKE'S OUT FRONT WAITING!

MIKE CAN JUST WAIT ONE GODDAMN MINUTE.

HE'S NEVER SEEN YOU WHEN YOU DON'T TAKE THESE, HAS HE? YOU THINK HE'D STILL LIKE YOU THEN? NOW SHUT UP AND TAKE YOUR FUCKING MEDICATION.

FUCK YOU, MOM!

GOD, I HATE IT WHEN YOU DO THAT!

GAK!

NICE WORK.

YOU LOVE ME, MIKE?

IT'S NOT GONNA BE EASY, YOU KNOW. OR PLEASANT.

BABY, I LOVE YOU TONS.

AND IT'S OKAY. THIS IS OUR NEW LIFE. LIFE IS *NEVER EASY OR PLEASANT*, RIGHT?

Yeah, tell me about it...

WELL, THAT'S WHAT'S GREAT ABOUT WHAT WE GOT.

WHATEVER HAPPENS, WE'LL BE IN IT *TOGETHER*.

SO WHAT HAPPENS NOW?

WHAT DO YOU MEAN?

WE KEEP HEADING TO THE CITY, RIGHT? LIKE WE PLANNED?

NO, THAT'S NOT WHAT I MEAN.

WHAT HAPPENS NOW WITH YOU? THIS IS JUST THE BEGINNING, RIGHT?

I MEAN, FUCK, YOU GOT THE SHAKES AND THE SWEATS AND I JUST SAW YOU PUKE FOR FIFTEEN MINUTES. I SAW BLOOD IN IT, MARIE.

I KNOW IT'S GONNA GET BAD. JUST TELL ME HOW BAD.

WAY WORSE. I KNOW THAT.

BUT EXACTLY HOW BAD? I DON'T KNOW. NO ONE KNOWS. THEY DON'T HAVE ANYTHING LIKE THIS ON FILE, THE DOCTORS SAY.

I TOLD YOU, I'M A FREAK.

LAST TIME I WENT OFF THE MEDS WAS WHEN I WAS FOURTEEN AND MY MOM DID SOMETHING TO PISS ME OFF. I LASTED SIX HOURS BEFORE I TOTALLY BLACKED OUT.

I JUST FLIPPED OUT. SHIT STARTED MOVING AROUND, LIKE FURNITURE AND PICTURES DROPPED OFF THE WALL. IT'S LIKE MY FUCKING BRAIN WAVES EXPLODED.

THE MEDS ARE BASICALLY JUST REALLY AMPED UP MOOD STABILIZERS, SOME CRAZY -DOSAGE, AND WITHOUT THEM MY HEAD JUST OVERLOADS.

I STARTED BLEEDING. FROM MY NOSE AND EARS AND THE SKIN SPLIT ON MY FOREHEAD. YOU CAN STILL SEE SCARS IF YOU LOOK CLOSE.

THEY SAY I ALMOST DIED. BUT I DUNNO.

THEY DON'T EVEN KNOW WHAT'S WRONG WITH ME, SO HOW DO THEY KNOW? ANYWAY, THAT WAS THREE YEARS AGO. I'VE BEEN WORKING ON CONTROLLING IT EVER SINCE.

WHAT DO YOU MEAN, CONTROLLING IT?

I TEST MYSELF. GO OFF THE MEDS A LITTLE, WAIT FOR THE SYMPTOMS, AND TRY TO CONTROL 'EM. I MEAN, I PUKE MY GUTS OUT EVERY TIME STILL, BUT I CAN KINDA CONTROL MY HEAD NOW.

I THINK.

YOU THINK?

I'VE NEVER LASTED BEYOND AN HOUR AND A HALF SINCE THEN. I HAVE TO BE CAREFUL. IF MY MOM CAUGHT ME DOING THIS, SHE SAID SHE'D HAVE ME INSTITUTIONALIZED.

SHE WANTS A NORMAL DAUGHTER, I GUESS. OR NO DAUGHTER AT ALL.

GAS·FOOD

SO SHE GETS NO DAUGHTER.

I'M SICK OF FEELING LIKE SOME SEMI-WANTED DRUGGED-UP LOSER PSYCHO FREAK.

ANYWAY. CAN WE GET GOING?

YOU BET.

WHAT CAN I DO? TELL ME WHAT I CAN DO TO HELP...

JUST DRIVE FASTER.

I'M ALREADY WAY OVER THE SPEED LIMIT. WE GET STOPPED, THE COPS WILL TAKE YOU RIGHT BACK HOME.

THERE'S NOTHING ELSE I CAN DO?

UHHHH...

MARIE?

LATER.

NEW YORK PABT

GAS

BUS TERMINU

2

"Emmy"

It's pretty easy not to talk much. Or at all. I don't go to school anymore, so there isn't too many people to talk to.

Working at the gas station is good 'cuz you don't need to explain anything to the people. Everyone knows how it goes. Most of them don't even notice I don't say anything.

My boss leaves me alone, mostly.

Most people leave me alone now.

They're afraid.

It's the trouble with a small town. Everyone knows too much about their neighbors.

Why they're afraid is the same reason I don't talk anymore.

I used to talk all the time. I liked making people do what I said. They always did what I said, no matter what.

I was much younger then, so it was fun. Until I got mad and I said something to my mom that I didn't mean and I couldn't take it back after I said it.

SKREEB

WHAT THE FUCK DID YOU DO?

No matter how hard I try sometimes stuff just comes out anyway.

THE END

3

FRANKLY, I'M SURPRISED ANYONE IN THIS FAMILY REMEMBERED I *EXISTED*, MUCH LESS THOUGHT TO INVITE ME TO THIS HORROR SHOW.

"MY FAMILY." HA. WHAT'S LEFT OF IT.

NEED A LIGHT?

THIS GUY HERE.

SEAN HURLEY. MY HALF-BROTHER.

MY *HOT FUCKING* HALF-BROTHER, WHO, IF HE *WASN'T* MY BROTHER, I'D BE ALL OVER IN A HEARTBEAT.

CHRIST, LAST TIME I SAW SEAN HE WAS ALL OF *SEVEN* AND PLAYED WITH MATCHBOX CARS. I CAN'T BELIEVE HE GREW UP INTO *THIS*.

PURE THOUGHTS, SAMANTHA. JUST KEEP TELLING YOURSELF: HE'S YOUR *BROTHER*.

YEAH, ME TOO. LEFT THE LIGHTER BACK IN THE CAR, THOUGH.

SO, WHADDYA SAY? HAD ENOUGH OF THIS MORBID, FUCKED-UP, SOCIALLY CONSTRUCTED BEREAVEMENT SHIT YET?

I DON'T KNOW ABOUT YOU, BUT I JUST WANNA GO DRIVE SOMEWHERE AND GET DRUNK.

LIKE, FOR A FUCKING *WEEK*.

OH YEAH, HE'S MY BROTHER ALL RIGHT.

LET'S GO.

"BAD BLOOD"

WELL, *THAT* WAS NICE AND PLEASANT.

WHAT WAS?

BY THE WAY, YOUR LIGHTER DOESN'T WORK FOR SHIT.

CHEAPEST BOX THEY HAD, NO SERVICE WHATSOEVER, AND IT WAS STILL *FIVE GRAND.* JUST TO LAY A FUCKING CORPSE IN THE GROUND.

CHRIST! YOU THINK THEY'D MAKE IT EASIER ON PEOPLE. WHAT, THEY WANT PEOPLE THAT CAN'T PAY JUST TOSSING CORPSES BY THE SIDE OF THE ROAD?

HEH.

THAT'S A GOOD IDEA. WE SHOULDA DONE THAT INSTEAD. STARTED A NEW THING.

BOOZE UP AND FUCKIN' RIOT.

TELL ME YOU GOT MATCHES. THIS THING IS *NOT WORKING.*

I GOT NOTHING. WE'LL MAKE A STOP.

OK, BUT HURRY UP. I'M JONESING HARD.

SEEING THAT *HOLE* IN THE GROUND... I DUNNO. I'M ALL SKETCHED OUT.

SKETCHED OUT? DO FUNERALS DO THAT TO YOU?

HOW THE FUCK SHOULD I KNOW? THAT WAS MY FIRST ONE. WHEN MY MOM KICKED, I PLAYED HOOKY AND GOT WASTED.

AND MY DAD WAS IN THAT CASKET... I DUNNO. I DON'T EVEN KNOW HIM, SEAN! AND I DON'T EVEN KNOW YOU, FOR THAT MATTER.

KINDA WEIRD.

YEAH.

WHEN YOU AND YOUR MOM MOVED AWAY, I WAS KINDA PISSED OFF ABOUT IT.

BUT WHAT ELSE COULD THEY DO? THEY HATED EACH OTHER, SAMANTHA, THEY WERE ALWAYS AT EACH OTHER'S THROATS. I DUNNO, I SAW MORE OF IT, I GUESS, CUZ I WAS OLDER.

BUT YOU HAD TO HAVE BEEN BETTER OFF, MOVING AWAY RATHER THAN STAYING HERE. IT WAS PRETTY FUCKING GRIM. A LOT OF UGLY SHIT WENT DOWN.

YOU WANNA TALK ABOUT GRIM AND UGLY? FUCK, SEAN. MY MOM DIED A YEAR AGO, AND I'VE BEEN LIVING AT THAT FUCKING SCHOOL.

I KNOW. YOU SENT ME A POSTCARD ONCE.

SUMMERS AND HOLIDAYS, I WAS THE ONLY KID THAT STAYED AT SCHOOL. DAD ACTUALLY PAID EXTRA FOR ME TO STAY THERE DURING THOSE TIMES.

JESUS CHRIST...

AND I REALLY FUCKING NEED TO SMOKE THIS CIGARETTE!

SUN. MANICURED LAWNS. GOLF COURSES. LUXURY AUTOMOBILES. WHITE PEOPLE.

HOME. WHERE THE RICH ASSHOLES ROAM, AND WHERE EVEN THE FUCKING CONVENIENCE STORES ARE PRETENTIOUS.

JON'S
MINI-MART

I WISH I COULD SAY I WAS NEVER FROM HERE.

HEY...

HEY SEAN, COME LOOK AT THIS!

FUCKING ASSHOLES WOULDN'T GIVE ME MATCHES UNLESS I BOUGHT SOMETHING.

WE USED TO COME HERE, AS KIDS, RIGHT? OUR NAMES ARE IN THE ASPHALT. DID *YOU* DO THAT, OR DID I?

OH YEAH, CHECK THAT OUT. YEAH, WE USED TO COME HERE ON OUR BIKES FOR CANDY, REMEMBER?

WHAT THE FUCK? DID YOU BUY SOMETHING THEN?

WE'RE DRIVING BACK HOME. I CAN REMEMBER THE ROUTE NOW.

BUT JUST BARELY.

NEVER THOUGHT I'D BE BACK HERE. I ALWAYS TOLD MYSELF THIS WAS THE LAST PLACE I WOULD EVER VISIT AGAIN.

I WAS COOL WITH THAT. AND THEN HERE I AM, DRAGGED BACK TO WATCH A DAD I NEVER REALLY KNEW BE BURIED. *NOT* IDEAL.

AT LEAST SEAN'S COOL.

IF I GOTTA HAVE A FAMILY AGAIN, I'M GLAD IT'S HIM.

THAT WAS KINDA WEIRD, HUH? SEEING OUR NAMES IN THE ASPHALT?

YOU WERE A FUCKING TERROR ON THAT DIRTBIKE YOU HAD.

YEAH. THAT BIKE.

ANOTHER LIFETIME.

SAMANTHA? WHAT'RE YOU LOOKING AT?

NOTHING. SEAN, WHAT DID YOU DO, YOU KNOW, GROWING UP?

WHAT?

WHAT WERE YOU LIKE IN SCHOOL? WHAT STUFF DID YOU DO? WHAT WAS DAD LIKE?

DON'T LOOK AT ME LIKE THAT. I'M NOT CRAZY. YOU'RE MY BROTHER, SEAN, AND I'M CURIOUS.

HAVEN'T SEEN YOU IN LIKE A DECADE. MORE THAN A DECADE.

I JUST WANNA KNOW WHO YOU ARE, SEAN.

OK, FAIR ENOUGH. I'LL TELL YOU SOMETHING.

DAD DROVE MY MOM AWAY, TOO, A FEW YEARS BEFORE THAT. I WAS PRETTY MAD AT HIM, SO I STARTED FUCKING UP AT SCHOOL, GETTING INTO FIGHTS, SHOPLIFTING, KID STUFF LIKE THAT.

OK. WHEN YOU AND YOUR MOM LEFT, I SORTA LOST IT.

AND I ALWAYS MADE SURE I GOT CAUGHT. I WANTED TO EMBARRAS THE OLD MAN. AND I DID, PLENTY OF TIMES, OVER AND OVER.

BUT I NEVER GOT THE REACTION I WANTED. I WANTED HIM MAD, I WANTED HIM TO BEAT ME UP, SOMETHING, I DUNNO. I WANTED HIM TO ACT LIKE THE ASSHOLE HE WAS IN MY MIND, TO VALIDATE MY ANGER.

BUT I JUST MADE HIM SAD.

THAT JUST MADE ME FEEL WORSE. MADE ME HATE HIM MORE.

SO I STOPPED WITH ALL THAT, AND SORTA WITHDREW. I WOULD STAY IN MY ROOM READING OR PLAYING GUITAR, OR STAY OVER AT A FRIEND'S. SOMETIMES WEEKS WOULD GO BY WITHOUT SEEING DAD.

THERE WAS THIS ONE TIME, I THINK AROUND THE TIME YOUR MOM DIED, I WAS GOING OUT TO A SHOW, AND HE STARTING ARGUING WITH ME ABOUT THE CAR. I THINK HE WAS DRUNK. IT GOT REALLY UGLY, I SAID A BUNCH OF REALLY HARSH SHIT, AND LEFT.

I GOT A MILE OR SO DOWN THE ROAD, AND REALIZED I HAD TO GO BACK. I FORGOT SOMETHING.

I WALK IN, AND DAD IS WATCHING TV AND CRYING HIS EYES OUT. REALLY BAWLING. IT WAS SOME STUPID HALLMARK AD ON TV OR SOMETHING. HE WAS JUST TOTALLY BREAKING DOWN.

I TOOK HIM UPSTAIRS TO GET HIM TO SLEEP IT OFF, AND HE STARTS *BABBLING*, TELLING ME ALL THIS STUFF, ABOUT YOUR MOM, MY MOM, *HIS* PARENTS, HOW FUCKED UP HE WAS, HOW HE SCREWED THINGS UP WITH ME...

AND APPARENTLY, HE'S BEEN TRYING TO *KILL HIMSELF* FOR YEARS, BUT HE JUST KEEPS FUCKING THAT UP TOO.

WHAT?

HOW?

I JUST LET HIM TALK. HE WENT ON FOR *HOURS*, UNTIL HE JUST FELL ASLEEP FROM EXHAUSTION, I GUESS. HE TOLD ME A LOT OF STUFF THAT NIGHT, ABOUT OUR FAMILY.

...

LIKE *WHAT?*

SAMANTHA, I KNOW YOU'RE PRETTY PISSED OFF AT DAD FOR A LOT OF SHIT, BUT AT THE RISK OF SOUNDING REALLY LAME, YOU GOTTA CUT HIM A BREAK.

I NEVER EXPECTED PERFECTION, SEAN. I WOULDN'T WANT THAT. I DON'T NEED THE HOUSE OR THE STATION WAGON OR THE PICKET FENCE AND RIDES TO SOCCER PRACTICE. THAT SORT OF SUBURBAN ROBOT SHIT, NO THANKS.

I WOULD HAVE SETTLED FOR HAVING A DAD AND A MOM THAT AT LEAST TRIED TO GET ALONG, AND A BIG BROTHER TO WATCH OUT FOR ME. BUT ALL I GOT WAS BOARDING SCHOOL AND EMPTY HOLIDAYS.

THAT WAS NEVER GONNA HAPPEN, SAMANTHA. DAD WASN'T THAT KIND OF DAD. HE NEVER WAS. IF YOU HAD STAYED, YOU WOULDN'T HAVE GOTTEN THAT FROM HIM.

I SAW INSIDE HIM THAT NIGHT. HE'S NOT A FATHER, HE'S JUST A FUCKED-UP GUY, NO BETTER OR WORSE THAN ANY OF US.

YOU GOTTA LET HIM HAVE THAT, SAMANTHA.

LET HIM BE HAPPY WITH THAT.

YEAH, WELL, LUCKY FOR HIM, HE'S DEAD.

HE'S GOT ETERNITY TO BE HAPPY, AND I'M STUCK HERE TO DEAL WITH IT.

snif

I'M SEVENTEEN YEARS OLD, SEAN, I'M PRACTICALLY AN ADULT! I FUCKING GREW UP WHEN I WAS *FIVE*, I HAD TO! I WAS *NEVER* A NORMAL KID, I NEVER GOT TO DO NORMAL KID SHIT.

I WAS FIVE WHEN I LEFT. YOU AND I USED TO BE BEST BUDS, SEAN.

AND NOW YOU'RE THIS COOL GUY, A MAN, AND I DON'T EVEN KNOW WHO YOU *ARE*. I DON'T EVEN KNOW WHO I AM MOST OF THE TIME!

I JUST WISH...

I JUST WISH IT COULD BE YOU AND ME AND DAD AGAIN. WE COULD START OVER. IT DOESN'T HAVE TO BE "NORMAL," BUT SOMETHING WOULD BE A START.

heh heh

WHAT THE FUCK'RE YOU GRINNING FOR?

I'M SERIOUS ABOUT THIS, SEAN!

I KNOW YOU ARE.

BUT WOULDN'T YOU RATHER BE TALKING TO DAD ABOUT THIS?

GASP!

OH MY GOD. OH MY GOD.

WHY DOESN'T THIS HURT?

WHY AM I FUCKING *STILL* ALIVE?

'CUZ YOU'RE A *HURLEY*, THAT'S WHY.

WE'RE NOT DEAD. OKAY.

HURLEYS DON'T DIE.

SEAN, YOU GOTTA EXPLAIN THIS. I GOT A FUCKING *TREE BRANCH* IN MY CHEST.

SOME OF US KIDS JUST AREN'T BORN THIS WAY. AND TO TELL YOU THE TRUTH, I WASN'T SURE ABOUT YOU EITHER.

I DUNNO, SAMANTHA. IT'S A FAMILY THING. ALWAYS BEEN THAT WAY.

EVERY SO OFTEN, SURE, SOMEONE *DIES*, BUT IT'S ALL BULLSHIT. KEEPING UP APPEARANCES, TAX REASONS, STUFF LIKE THAT. WE ALWAYS BURY EMPTY CASKETS.

BUT NO ONE *REALLY* DIES. NOT EVEN DAD.

HE WASN'T SURE, Y'KNOW, ABOUT YOU, CUZ WHEN YOU WERE YOUNG YOU WERE SO MUCH LIKE YOUR MOM.

BUT AFTER SEEING YOU TODAY...

SAMANTHA--

YOU ARE *100% FUCKING HURLEY.*

DAD'S TOTALLY GONNA LOVE THIS.

4

ONE BIG STEP TOWARDS GROWING UP, JAMES, WOULD BE TO STOP GETTING *DRUNK* EVERY WEEKEND WITH THOSE "FRIENDS" OF YOURS.

THINK ABOUT IT!

Yeah, yeah...

SEE YOU LATER, DAD!

McKINNEY'S
BEER · PARTS · POOL

"Stand Strong"

THIRTY-SIX HOURS EARLIER.

YOU AREN'T READY YET?

THE GUYS'LL BE HERE ANY MINUTE.

I KNOW.

I DON'T HAVE TO DO THIS, YOU KNOW. WE DON'T NEED THE MONEY. WE GET BY OK.

OH, NO, OF COURSE YOU'RE RIGHT. WE DON'T NEED THE MONEY. WE DON'T STARVE, IF THAT'S WHAT YOU'RE SAYING.

BUT AT THE SAME TIME, I DON'T NEED TO WORK 12-HOUR SHIFTS WAITRESSING LIKE I FUCKING DO, AND I DON'T NEED TO SIT HOME ALONE ON NIGHTS AND WEEKENDS WHILE YOU PULL EXTRA SHIFTS AND THEN COME HOME STINKING AND TOO EXHAUSTED TO DO ANYTHING BUT WATCH TV.

IF YOU WANT THIS TO WORK BETWEEN US, SHOW SOME FUCKING INITIATIVE. I AM NOT GONNA LIVE LIKE OUR PARENTS DO.

WAIT, WHAT ABOUT MY PARENTS?

WHAT ABOUT THEM?

OH, JAMES, LEAVE IT ALONE, WOULD YA?

SO SICK OF HAVING THIS CONVERSATION.

I JUST DON'T SEE WHAT'S SO WRONG WITH MY PARENTS. THEY'VE ALWAYS BEEN GOOD, HONEST--

SNAP SNAP

SNAP

JAMES. WAKE UP. YOU SOUND LIKE YOUR DAD AGAIN.

LOOK AROUND YOU. LOOK AT THIS HOUSE. THIS ISN'T A FUCKING FAIRY TALE, THIS KIND OF LIFE.

WE'RE POOR. IT FUCKING SUCKS. THIS TOWN SUCKS, AND OUR JOBS SUCK.

NOW, GO DO SOMETHING ABOUT IT.

BVVRRMMMM

...THE PAYROLL IS JUST SITTIN' THERE, MAN, READY TO BE HANDED OUT MONDAY. JUST *SITTIN'* THERE!

WHAT DO YOU THINK, JIMMY? I FIGURE AN EASY SIXTY GRAND.

I THINK WE SHOULDN'T BE RIPPING OFF OUR OWN PAYROLL. YOU WANT ME TO HELP RIP OFF MY OWN FAMILY, MY DAD AND GRANDPA?

OH, COME ON, JIMMY. YOU KNOW IT'S INSURED. AND BESIDES, UNTIL PAYDAY IT'S STILL THE COMPANY'S MONEY.

WHAT?

OH, DON'T BE SUCH A FUCKING GOODY-GOODY. INSURANCE'LL PAY UP. YOUR DAD'LL GET HIS CHECK ON MONDAY. EVERYONE WILL.

HAH, YEAH! EVEN US! PAID *TWICE!*

HAHAHA!

SO GUYS, EVERYTHING COOL?

OH COME ON, JIMMY.

FUCK YOU.

YOU DON'T GET TO USE ME LIKE THIS. NOT ANYMORE, NOT SINCE LAST TIME.

JIMMY.

I KNOW THINGS WITH US HAVEN'T BEEN 100% COOL FOR A WHILE. IT'S OK, WE'RE GETTING OLDER, AND THAT CREW MENTALITY SHIT IS FOR KIDS. PEOPLE CHANGE, MOVE ON.

THIS ISN'T ABOUT THAT. THIS IS ABOUT MONEY, MAKING OUR LIVES A LITTLE BETTER, GETTING ONE OVER ON THE SYSTEM.

YOU KNOW THE PINK SLIPS ARE COMING REAL SOON, AND WHO DO YOU THINK THEY'LL LAY OFF FIRST?

US. THE YOUNG GUYS WITH NO FAMILY AND NO SENIORITY. THEN WHAT DO WE DO FOR MONEY IN THIS TOWN?

"BIG JIMMY THE UTENSIL."

GOOD TO HAVE ON YOUR SIDE WHEN YOU NEED DIRTY WORK DONE, BUT NOT WORTH RISKING YOUR OWN SELVES FOR, RIGHT?

HEY, JIMMY...

IT'S JAMES.

LET'S GET THIS OVER WITH.

FUCK.

IT'S BUILT IN. I WAS KINDA HOPING TO TAKE IT WITH US, CUT IT OPEN BACK AT MY BROTHER'S SHOP.

SO WHAT DO WE DO THEN? THE GUARD COMES BACK ON DUTY IN A FEW MINUTES.

A FEW MINUTES? WHAT THE FUCK?

IT WAS ALL I COULD BRIBE HIM FOR. SO WHAT ARE WE GONNA DO? WE CAN'T GET THIS DESK ALL THE WAY BACK TO THE TRUCK, CAN WE?

OH, FOR FUCK'S SAKE.

BAM

BAM

SOME FUCKING CREW YOU ALL ARE.

UH, WE CAN'T TAKE THAT ALL THE WAY TO THE TRUCK, YOU KNOW. WHAT ABOUT THE GATES? EVEN YOU CAN'T GET IT THROUGH THE GRILLE WORK...

"EVEN ME"?

DON'T WORRY, WE AREN'T TAKING IT THAT FAR.

FUCK!

WHAT THE FUCK DIDYA DO THAT FOR, JIMMY?

BANG

BANG

BANG

BANG

SHIT! THIS NOISE! --THE NIGHT SHIFT'LL HEAR FOR SURE!

OH WE ARE SO FUCKED!

WHAT THE FUCK'RE YOU SMILING FOR?

YOU KNOW WE GOT LAID OFF, JIMMY. THEY *KNOW* IT'S US THAT DID IT, BUT THEY CAN'T PROVE IT. SO THEY FIRED US.

AND WE DIDN'T GET THE MONEY.

I KNOW.

"YOU *KNOW*"? THAT'S ALL YOU HAVE TO SAY?

WHERE THE *FUCK* HAVE YOU BEEN?

DON'T COME HOME ANYMORE, AMY. I DON'T WANT TO LIVE WITH YOU.

YOU'RE *DUMPING* ME? *ME*?

JIMMY, YOU BIG DUMB UGLY *FUCKHEAD*! DON'T YOU FUCKING *DARE* WALK AWAY!

IT'S JAMES. JAMES McMURRAY.

AND I WILL NEVER HAVE TO HEAR ANY OF YOU SAY ANOTHER BAD THING ABOUT THAT NAME, AGAIN.

SLAM!

HEY.

JAMES! CHANGED YOUR MIND, EH? HAVE A SEAT, WE GOT TIME FOR ONE MORE.

A BEER OVER HERE FOR MY SON! CELEBRATE YOUR PROMOTION, RIGHT?

I CAN TELL HE'S YER BOY. SPITTING IMAGE, OF THE BOTH OF YA.

THE END.

5

SO I WORK IN THE STACKS. SO WHAT? YOU THINK I'M SOME KIND OF NERDY LIBRARY GIRL OR SOMETHING?

THAT I WEAR GLASSES ON A CHAIN AND SHIRTS BUTTONED ALL THE WAY UP AND I READ ALL THESE OBSCURE ARTSY BOOKS AND I AM SOME REPRESSED HORNY *ANIMAL* JUST WAITING FOR YOU TO COME ALONG AND SET ME FREE?

YOU THINK THAT'S WHAT I AM, DON'T YOU?

YOU THINK YOU *KNOW* ME LIKE THAT?

UM, *NO!* I DIDN'T MEAN--

NKSHOT!

FUCK YOU. SO TYPICAL.

ONE LOOK AND YOU THINK YOU GOT ME ALL FIGURED OUT. I'M *NOT* WHO YOU WANT ME TO BE.

NO! HEY, COME *BACK!* I JUST WANTED TO ASK YOU OUT FOR *COFFEE* OR SOMETHING! THAT'S ALL!

SHIT.

SPACE TRASH

I DON'T KNOW WHY I BOTHER COMING OUT. WHAT A WASTE OF MY TIME.

I KEEP HOPING NOT EVERYONE OUT THERE IS THE SAME, THAT I'LL FINALLY MEET SOMEONE THAT'S DIFFERENT, NOT LIKE THE REST OF THE ASSHOLES.

BIG MISTAKE.

FUCK, THERE ARE SOME SICK PEOPLE AT THIS PARTY.

"Girl You Want"

HI, KATE.

LOOKING LOVELY TONIGHT AS USUAL.

BUT THEN, EVERYONE THINKS SO, DON'T THEY?

SHFF

HEY, THAT WAS FUNNY.

THAT HIDING YOUR FACE THING YOU JUST DID, WITH YOUR HOOD. WHAT, ARE YOU WANTED BY THE LAW OR SOMETHING?

HUH.

WOW.

WELL, YOU'RE BUSY STUDYING.

LET ME KNOW IF YOU NEED A REFILL OR ANYTHING.

Wow. Finally.

She *saw* me.

Monday, March 22. 8:14pm

I'll be 20 years old in two months. And in all my life, only *one person* has ever seen me for *me*. And I met her just now at Starbucks.

I think I'm in love.

Tuesday, March 23. 6:45 am

She isn't in yet.

First some background: I used to think I was just nuts, that it was all in my head.

STAR COFFEE

I started carrying around my mirror to prove to myself that yes, something physical was *actually* happening to me.

Sometimes that just made me feel worse.

People see what they want to see in people, what they expect based on appearances or clothes or what kind of job they have. They fill in the blanks without even knowing that's what they're doing. I guess that's normal, right?

Tuesday, March 23, 9:12 am

HEY THERE! REMEMBER ME?

LOST HIGHWAY

HI! UM... OH YEAH, YOU'RE THE GIRL FROM YESTERDAY, RIGHT? WITH THE HOODIE? WHAT CAN I GET YOU?

UM... NOTHING.

SO YOU LIKE DAVID LYNCH?

...WHAT?

LOST HIGHWAY

I NEVER SAW IT, BUT I LIKED TWIN PEAKS.

OH, NO. THIS ISN'T FROM THE MOVIE. IT'S A *RECORD LABEL* I LIKE.

OH. I THOUGHT IT WAS THE *MOVIE*. 'CUZ I THOUGHT IF IT *WAS* MAYBE WE COULD RENT IT *SOMETIME* 'CUZ I'VE NEVER SEEN IT.

WHAT'D YOU SAY?

HEY, ARE YOU GONNA ORDER OR NOT? PEOPLE ARE WAITING!

SHUT THE FUCK UP!

Oh, no...

WHAT THE HELL WAS THAT ALL ABOUT?

I DON'T KNOW. I DON'T EVEN *KNOW* HER.

124

Thursday, March 25. 10:17 pm

It's been two days.
48 hours.
Since last contact.

They closed seventeen minutes
ago. Three minutes until she locks
up. Then she gets on the bus.

I dunno...

I just know.

How do I know?

You just don't know what it's like, being judged all the time. People are sick, they want you to be sick fucking things sometimes.

Or if not that then they want you to be something you just *aren't*, even though you might *wish* you could be. That's *worse*.

But she's not like that. She's-- she...

Oh my God, I don't even know her name...

Doesn't matter.

She'll tell me her name when the time is right. She'll tell me hers and I'll tell her mine.

Kate.

Katie, Kath, Kat. Is that short for Katherine? With a "k" or a "c"?

Even my name is what people want it to be.

I bet she has a cool name. Interesting and kinda unusual like "Gretchen" or "Miranda" or "Tatiana," something like that.

I hate my name but I bet I'll like it when she says it.

GOOD JOB, KATE. YOU BLEW IT. STUPID.

EVERYONE THINKS SO.

THE END

6

"What You Wish For"

I TRY TO FORGET, BUT THE MEMORIES NEVER FADE.

I REMEMBER HOW NEW IT SEEMED, THE HOUSES, THE LANDSCAPING, THE CARS IN THE NEIGHBORS' DRIVEWAYS. BRAND NEW HOMES, NEW FAMILIES, FULL OF HOPE AND POWER.

I GUESS THAT'S THE AMERICAN DREAM.

GET ONE UP ON EVERYONE ELSE.

I HATED IT. EVERYONE WAS SO WHITE AND BLONDE. EVERYTHING TAN AND CHROME AND GLEAMING.

I HATED HOW I DIDN'T FIT IN.

THE ONLY PERSON THAT LOOKED LIKE ME WEEDED THE NEIGHBOR'S LAWN.

I NEVER KNEW HIS NAME, BUT HE ALWAYS MADE ME FEEL BETTER SOMEHOW.

THEN THERE WAS MY MOM.

I KNOW SHE TRIED.

BUT SHE WAS JUST AS MISERABLE AND ANGRY AND OUT OF PLACE AS I WAS.

DINNERTIME.

DAD TALKING ABOUT HIS BORING JOB.

AGAIN.

DAD WAS OK.

HE WAS IN THE NAVY AND MET MY MOM OVERSEAS.

WE GOT ALONG GREAT, I JUST WONDER IF HE KNEW WHAT HE WAS GETTING INTO WHEN HE MARRIED HER.

BUT I KNOW DAD TRIED TOO.

hee hee

IT JUST WASN'T ENOUGH, I GUESS.

COFFUCIOUS SAY

ONE DAY IT JUST GOT TO BE TOO MUCH, FOR ALL OF US.

I GOT SAD.

MOM CRIED.

DAD GOT *SUPER* MAD.

THEN I GOT SCARED AND EMBARRASSED.

THE WHOLE NEIGHBORHOOD JUST HATED US MORE.

THAT NIGHT, THINKING ABOUT IT, MY STOMACH WAS SICK. HAVING YOUR PARENTS FIGHT YOUR BATTLES JUST MADE IT WORSE FOR YOU LATER.

THEY NEVER GET THAT.

HUH?

PUPPY?

PUPPY?

HEY, YOU!

GET THE *HELL* OUT OF MY YARD, OR YOU'LL END UP LIKE YOUR FUCKIN' DOG!

...PUPPY?

I'm sorry, I tried to stop him--

FUCKIN' THING DUG AND SHAT IN MY YARD ALL THE GODDAMN TIME.

YOU *NEEDED* TO KEEP A BETTER EYE ON IT.

ALL THE WHILE, I NEVER GOT MAD LIKE MY MOM AND DAD.

SAD, UPSET, BUT NEVER ANGRY. I GUESS I JUST TOOK IT. *ABSORBED* IT.

I ALWAYS HAD MY DOG THERE, TO CHILL ME OUT AND MAKE ME FEEL BETTER.

BUT THEY KILLED HIM.

AND THEN I GOT MAD.

IT ALL CAME OUT, EVERYTHING I HELD IN.

AND AS MUCH AS MY DOG ONCE HELPED CONTROL MY ANGER, HE NOW HELPED *FOCUS* IT.

I NEEDED AMPLIFICATION.

A LOT OF HATE, A LOT OF ANGER.

FOR MOM, FOR DAD, FOR ME.

I COULD FEEL IT, THE FEAR AND HURT TURNING TO RAGE.

JUST LIKE THAT, IT WAS OVER.

MY DOG WAS OK. I FELT CALM AGAIN.

NOT MAD ANYMORE.

I REMEMBER THAT DAY WELL ENOUGH.

THE ONE DAY I LOST CONTROL, THE ONE DAY I GOT MAD. THE *ONE* DAY I LET THOSE FEELINGS OUT.

DID THEY DESERVE IT?

YOU OK, KEN?

YOU WANNA DRIVE A BIT? SHOW ME AROUND?

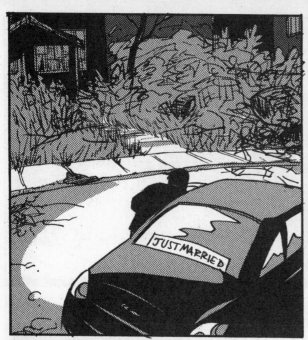

JUST MARRIED

NAH, NOTHING MUCH TO SEE.

WOW, IT'S REALLY KIND OF A MESS. WHAT HAPPENED? IT LOOKS LIKE IT WAS A NICE NEIGHBORHOOD.

LOTS OF ROOM TO RUN AROUND AND PLAY.

KEN?

I DUNNO. IT WAS A LONG TIME AGO.

I CAN'T REMEMBER.

THE END

7

"One Shot, Don't Miss"

THE END

8

Oh my god.

"Mixtape"

BUT WE GO HERE ALL THE TIME.

NO WE *DON'T*, NICK.

THINK BACK.

...I GUESS YOU USUALLY MEET ME HERE, AND WE GO SOMEWHERE ELSE. OR WE JUST GO HOME.

WHEN YOU'RE READY TO GO, YES.

SO WHERE DO *I* LIKE TO GO WHEN WE GO OUT?

DO YOU KNOW?

217

THE END

9

GOT YOU A COFFEE, GABE.

COOL.

YOU'RE WELCOME, GABE.

WHAT?

WHAT?

OH, NEVER MIND.

"Breaking Up"

THAT WAS BACK THEN.

HEY, IT'S AFTER MIDNIGHT. IT'S ANOTHER DAY.

DOES THIS NOW COUNT AS A SECOND DATE?

HA HA, SURE, WHY NOT?

YOU KNOW I NEVER DO THIS.

YEAH, YEAH, I KNOW, THAT'S THE BIGGEST CLICHÉ IN THE WORLD.

IT IS.

But it's true.

226

FUCK. COME ON, LIGHT.

WHAT THE HELL ARE *YOU* LOOKING AT?

OH, MR. PIPPER AND I DON'T LIKE SMOKE IN HERE. SORRY. IT GETS IN HIS FUR AND EVERYTHING.

I HAVE TO DO THIS OUT HERE. THE LIGHT SUCKS IN THE BATHROOM AND IF I DON'T DO THIS RIGHT I'LL LOOK RETARDED.

WHAT AM I DOING HERE?

NOW.

WELL?

WHAT?

YOU TELL ME; YOU INVITED ME OUT TO THIS STUPID PLACE ON A SATURDAY.

LOOK, IT'S CLEAR I DO NOTHING THESE DAYS BUT PISS YOU OFF. SO WHAT, YOU TAKE ME HERE TO DUMP ME?

"DUMP" YOU? DON'T ACT LIKE YOU'RE IN HIGH SCHOOL, GABE.

WHAT, YOU ARE DUMPING ME?

HERE?

BE QUIET.

SO WHY HERE? WHY IN PUBLIC?

SO I WOULDN'T FREAK OUT?

A LOT OF GOOD THAT WOULD DO! LOOK AT YOU, FREAKING OUT!

MANIPULATIVE. REAL NICE. THANKS; TREAT ME LIKE I'M FIVE.

LOOK, GABE, CAN'T WE TRY AND MAKE THIS CIVIL, AT LEAST? I DON'T SEE ANY REASON TO END THIS ANGRY.

COME ON. YOU CAN'T TELL ME YOU DIDN'T SEE THIS COMING.

BACK THEN.

HEY.

HEY ANGIE. YOU AWAKE?

COME ON, WAKE UP.

GOD.

I DON'T KNOW WHY I EVEN BOTHER COMING OVER.

230

GABE...

YOU CAN'T TELL ME YOU'VE BEEN HAPPY.

WHAT'RE YOU TALKING ABOUT? I'M HAPPY.

WHAT?

WELL, YEAH, IT HASN'T BEEN PERFECT FOR A WHILE. BUT YOU SAID THAT WAS BECAUSE OF THAT THING AT YOUR WORK, BUT IT WOULD GET BETTER. I FIGURED I JUST HAD TO WAIT.

YOU ASKED ME TO DO THAT.

YEAH, I KNOW I DID.

I NEEDED YOUR SUPPORT. I DON'T REALLY THINK I GOT IT, GABE. I GUESS I RESENT YOU FOR THAT.

WHAT ARE YOU TALKING ABOUT? DIDN'T YOU JUST SAY IT WASN'T YOUR JOB TO MAKE ME FEEL GOOD?

OH, THAT IS NOT THE SAME THING.

DON'T TRY TO TURN THIS AROUND ON ME.

WAY BACK AT THE BEGINNING.

SO, A PHOTOGRAPHIC MEMORY, HUH?

WELL, NOT A PHOTOGRAPHIC MEMORY PER SE, BUT I DO HAVE THIS SPOOKY ABILITY TO REMEMBER THINGS PEOPLE SAY, FOREVER.

MMM HMMM.

SO IF I SAY I REALLY WANT TO LEARN GUITAR BUT THEN I GET LAZY AND FORGET...

...YOU'LL REMIND ME TO PRACTICE?

SURE, IF YOU WANT ME TO.

AND IF I TELL YOU I LIKE TULIPS...

...YOU'LL STILL BUY THEM FOR ME WHEN I'M AN OLD WOMAN?

YEP.

AND IF I TOLD YOU I LOVE YOU FOREVER...

...YOU'LL NEVER EVER FORGET THAT FOR AS LONG AS YOU LIVE, RIGHT?

ANGIE...

NEVER EVER, FOR AS LONG AS I LIVE.

I PROMISE.

235

NOW.

SO WE'RE REALLY BREAKING UP, THEN?

DO YOU SEE ANOTHER SOLUTION?

YOU KNOW...

...I'M REALLY SORRY I DID ALL THOSE THINGS. SORRY FOR NOT BEING BETTER ABOUT STUFF.

THANKS, GABE.

REALLY. I'M SORRY.

THANKS.

BACK THEN.

YOU KNOW WHAT?

WHAT?

YOU ARE SO LUCKY.

I AM, AM I? TELL ME WHY.

'CUZ I'M THE PERFECT GIRLFRIEND.

OH YEAH? YOU THINK SO, HUH?

YOU DON'T THINK SO?

WHAT? WHAT DID I DO? I WAS JUST PLAYING!

THANKS FOR RUINING THE DAY, ASSHOLE.

GABE?

...HEY. WHAT'S GOING ON?

GABE.

WHO IS "DEVILGRRL82"?

AND WHY DID SHE EMAIL YOU HER PICTURE?

NOW.

GABE, I GOTTA GO.

WHAT DO YOU MEAN?

I HAVE SOME STUFF TO DO.

SO IS THAT IT?

PLEASE, ANGIE.

GABE...

WHAT ARE YOU SAYING PLEASE FOR? WHAT DO YOU WANT?

DO YOU REALLY WANT TO STAY TOGETHER?

THINK ABOUT IT. IS THAT REALLY GOING TO MAKE YOU HAPPY?

ANGIE--

NO, REALLY THINK ABOUT IT A MINUTE.

242

WELL?

...WILL WE STILL TALK?

SURE. I MEAN, IF YOU WANT TO.

I THINK I'D LIKE THAT.

I STILL LOVE YOU, YOU KNOW.

I LOVE YOU TOO, GABE.

10

WHAT?

WHAT?

IS SOMETHING WRONG?

WHAT?

YES, THAT'S ALL YOU'VE BEEN SAYING FOR THE LAST 30 SECONDS, DEAR.

I'M GOING OUT FOR A SMOKE.

"Damaged"

I FEEL SO EXPOSED.

NOT SO BAD ONCE YOU GET USED TO IT.

BESIDES, IT'S NO PICNIC BEING PRIVY TO ALL YOUR DAMAGE, YOU KNOW.

MY "DAMAGE." GEE, THANKS.

MY PLEASURE.

YOU WANT ANOTHER ONE?

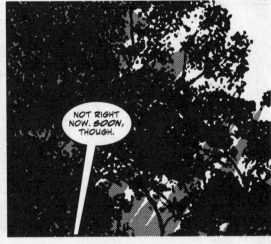

NOT RIGHT NOW. *SOON*, THOUGH.

...SO I JUST DON'T GET IT. WHAT DID I DO WRONG THERE? SHE NEVER CALLED BACK.

WELL, HOW MANY MESSAGES DID YOU LEAVE?

JUST A COUPLE.

OK, OK, I LEFT SIX MESSAGES.

NINE MESSAGES.

YEAH, BUT WHAT'S THAT?

GOOD QUESTION.

HAVE A LITTLE FAITH, MAN. YOU'RE NOT *THAT* CREEPY A DUDE; DO YOURSELF A FAVOR AND STOP ACTING LIKE YOU ARE.

JUST BE YOURSELF.

YOU KNOW THAT'S TOTALLY *CRAZY,* RIGHT?

I'LL COME FIND YOU AGAIN TOMORROW, MAYBE.

SURE YOU DON'T WANT A CAB?

NAH, I LIKE THE TRAIN.

OK. WELL, HERE YOU GO.

YOU DON'T NEED TO KEEP DOING THIS. I TOLD YOU, I'M NOT A THERAPIST. AND YOU GIVE ME SO MUCH MONEY, IT'S CRAZY.

I KNOW, BUT YOU'VE HELPED ME ANYWAY. THE PAST TWO WEEKS HAVE BEEN SO MUCH BETTER. I FEEL IT'S THE LEAST I COULD DO.

OK. WELL, I APPRECIATE IT. I COULDN'T REALLY LIVE WITHOUT IT, TO BE HONEST.

OK, OFF I GO. SEE YA! HAVE FUN AT THE GYM!

BYE! TAKE CARE!

265

WHAT THE HELL?

THAT'S *HER*. WHAT IS SHE DOING? WHERE IS SHE GOING? SHE LIVES IN BROOKLYN...

HEY DRIVER! FOLLOW THAT CAB!

WE GOT A RED LIGHT, BOSS. THEY'RE ALREADY GONE.

N.Y.C. TAXI

WEIRD.

HEY DRIVER, JUST TAKE ME HOME INSTEAD. SIXTY-FIRST AND COLUMBUS.

That's supposed to be empty, that apartment...

What the fuck?

HELLO? IT'S YOUR NEIGHBOR. ANYONE HOME?

WHAT A DAY FOR RAIN, EH?

MRS. MARTIN--

HE WAS ALWAYS A MESS, TOMMY WAS, AND I WAS ALWAYS AMAZED HE MANAGED TO ACCOMPLISH WHAT HE DID.

HE WAS A MISERABLE KID, A BULLY, TORTURING THE STRAYS IN OUR NEIGHBORHOOD, STEALING FROM ME, YOU NAME IT. BAD GRADES, HORRIBLE ATTITUDE. IT'S NO WONDER HE NEVER HAD ANY FRIENDS.

I BREATHED A SIGH OF RELIEF WHEN HE LEFT FOR COLLEGE, AND ANOTHER WHEN IT SEEMED LIKE HE EVENED OUT A BIT.

BUT I HAVEN'T SPOKEN TO HIM IN FIVE YEARS, AND NOW HE'S DEAD.

MRS. MARTIN, TOMMY HAD A LOT OF PROBLEMS, BUT HE WAS WORKING ON IT, HE WAS GETTING BETTER. HE NEEDED SOME HELP, THAT'S ALL.

I KNOW HE FELT BAD ABOUT BEING OUT OF CONTACT FOR SO LONG, AND HE WAS GOING TO CALL YOU SOON. HE WAS VERY SORRY FOR SHUTTING YOU OUT FOR SO LONG.

I KNOW FOR A FACT HE LOVED YOU VERY MUCH, MRS. MARTIN.

THE END

11

"Midnight to Six"

MANAGER

WHAT "ERROR"? JUST *SEND*, GODDAMN IT!

ISN'T THIS JUST A *TELEPHONE*? HOW HARD IS IT TO DIAL A NUMBER?

EH?

HELLO? SOMEONE THERE?

HELLO BRADLEY.

WHAT ARE YOU *DOING*, BRADLEY?

JACE! JESUS CHRIST, YOU FUCKIN' SCARED ME--

GAH! OW! FUCK!

WHAM

DON'T THINK YOU'LL BE NEEDING THESE.

SWIPE

Well, this just keeps getting better and better.

JILL!

THE END

12

Colorfade my vision from the sun too bright
Remembering what we did to each other
Thinking of you and my mind goes white
Brooklyn mornings upstate nights

Driving in silence but I like it just fine
Turnpike thruway heading due north
Back to the city is it already that time?
Wrapped in smells of woodsmoke and life

Sharing the leaves
Caught in your hair
Sharing the words
Floating away

Sharing the silence
That brings us together
Back home to Brooklyn
Start of the week

Heavy feet walking subway stair stomping
Breath held tight against subway car heat

Your body feels light and your T-shirt back's sticking
You're here for a reason you can't just be leaving

Your heart may be free and your life is your own
Your soul is my soul clenched in my fist

Drifting apart won't find me alone
Moving away from standing still stone

Pinch me or hit me this can't be my life

I'm only twenty-eight and I slept at least nine

It's not the city or family that's wrong or not right
A lifetime of love and exploring and strife

Leaving with you

Leaving as one

Too much like death

Meeting you later
Promise you'll be there

Your eyes feel like home

And that's all that I'll need

I know it takes courage I think that I could

Never be no, babe, I'm ready to go

From a rooftop in Brooklyn to sleepwalking on air

From twenty-eight years to my last night with you

Mon dernier jour avec toi and I'll be with you forever

"Mon Dernier Jour Avec Toi"
(My Last Night With You)

THE END

I thought up DEMO back in 2002 in a car in upstate New York. I had spent some time a few years before writing teen superheroes for Marvel Comics, and I wanted to take a stab at something similar, but something I would have more control over, to interpret the concept of "young people with power" the way I wanted to. My first ideas weren't too far removed from standard comic book stereotypes, but as I sat down and began to write the scripts, the concept evolved. My definition of "superpowers" changed to more universal ideas about power and control, the characters grew up from rebellious teenagers to complex people in their twenties and thirties. Becky and I spent eighteen months with DEMO, ending the series with something completely different from when we started. This spontaneous creative evolution is one of my favorite things about DEMO.

The other would be Becky Cloonan's incredible range and versatility. She'll act nonchalant about it, but speaking as an illustrator myself, being able to switch styles as she did is a rare gift that few of us possess. I'll always feel honored to have her as a collaborator and a friend.

And even though DEMO was originally created as monthly serialized comics, collecting them into a single volume as short stories keeps them available for the long term, and if you're picking up DEMO for the first time, I hope you enjoy reading it as much as we did creating it.

Brian Wood

This book is a collection of 18 months of my life. It's so surreal; when I look back on each story I can remember exactly where I was and what I was feeling when I drew each page. I hope this collection brings back memories for everyone; the store that you bought a particular issue at, where you were when you read it, the people you lent your copies to and never got back...

I learned so much from working on this comic, and also from working with Brian. I learned things that stick with you, the kind of things that you will use for the rest of your life. I think of DEMO as a turning point, and I look back with fondness on every panel that I drew.

Becky Cloonan

Amy ♥ L. ARM

Jimmy ♥

extra thugs

FRIEND #2

LEADER

FRIEND #1

BLOOD FOR BLOOD

4

5

6

7

8

9

10

11

12